APPLEWOOD's
PICTORIAL AMERICA

BOOKS

APPLEWOOD BOOKS
Carlisle, Massachusetts

TABLE OF
Contents

[N⁰· 1 THE LIBRARY OF CONGRESS.]

[N⁰· 2 CLOSED BOOK ON LAP OUTSIDE
THE NATIONAL ARCHIVES.]

[N⁰· 3 CHERUB WITH OPEN BOOK
AT THE SUPREME COURT.]

[N⁰· 4 THE LIBRARY OF CONGRESS READING ROOM IN ROTUNDA.]

[*N⁰.* 5 SIBYL HOLDING A TABLET.]

[*N⁰.* 6 THE GUTENBERG BIBLE.]

[*N⁰.* 7 HOMER AND PLATO.]

Moses.

[$N^o.$ 8 MOSES AND THE TEN COMMANDMENTS.]

[$N^o.$ 9 THE BIBLE.]

[$N^o.$ 10

TEXT FROM THE KORAN.]

[*Nos.* 13–14 **THE LIBRARY.**]

[*Nos.* 15–16 **THE LIBRARY.**]

[*N⁰.* 17 THE BOSTON PUBLIC LIBRARY.]

[*N⁰.* 18 BATES HALL—BOSTON FREE LIBRARY.]

[*No.* 19 THE NEW YORK PUBLIC LIBRARY.]

[*No.* 20 CARD CATALOG AT THE LIBRARY OF CONGRESS.]

[N⁰· 21   READING THE NEWS—OFF DUTY.]

[N⁰· 22   LINCOLN READING THE BIBLE TO HIS SON.]

[N⁰· 23
DAGUERREOTYPE
OF A WOMAN
HOLDING A BOOK.]

[N⁰ˢ· 24–25   CIVIL WAR PHOTOGRAPH BOOK.

CARDNER'S PHOTOGRAPHIC SKETCH BOOK OF THE WAR.

PHOTOGRAPHIC SKETCH BOOK OF THE WAR.

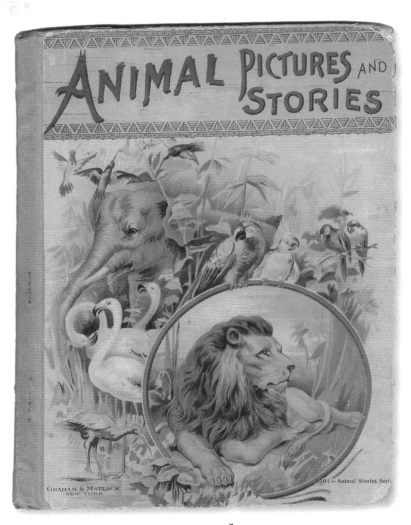

[*N*⁰· 26 AN OLD CHILDREN'S BOOK.]

[*N*⁰ˢ· 27–28 GARGOYLES.]

[№· 29 RELIEF OF SCHOOLROOM SCENE.]

[№· 30 CURRIER & IVES PRINT.]

[*No.* 31 TWO YOUNG GIRLS READING A BOOK.]

[*Nos.* 32–34 READERS.]

[*N⁰.* 35 READING.]

[*Nos.* 36–38 **READING.**]

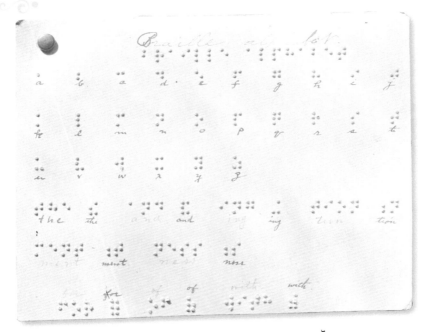

[*No.* 39   BRAILLE: THE ALPHABET FOR THE BLIND.]

[*No.* 40   HELEN KELLER WITH A BRAILLE BOOK.]

STIRRING TIMES IN AUSTRIA DESCRIBED BY MARK TWAIN

IN HARPER'S MARCH

[No. 41 BOOK ADVERTISEMENT.]

[*N⁰.* 42 EARLY BOOK ADVERTISEMENT.]

[*N⁰·* 43 VINTAGE BOOK COVER.]

[No. 44
THE OLD CORNER BOOKSTORE.]

[No. 45
SLEEPING CAT IN A BOOKSHOP.]

[N⁰. 46 COVER FEATURING A BOOKSELLER.]

[*N⁰.* 47   OLD MAN READING A BIBLE.]

[*N⁰.* 48
TITLE PAGE IMAGE
SHOWING TWO
READERS.]

[Nº 49 RELIGIOUS BOOKS BUILD CHARACTER.]

[*N⁰.* 50 POSTER FROM THE EARLY 1900s.]

[N°. 51 POSTER FROM THE EARLY 1920s.]

[Nº. 52   WWI POSTER.]

[*Nº.* 54 WORKS PROGRESS ADMINISTRATION POSTER.]

Little
Miss Muffet...

••• sat on a tuffet
reading a picture book
there came a spider—
and sat down beside her
and said, "May I have a look"?

MADE BY ILLINOIS WPA ART PROJECT-CHICAGO

[*No.* 55 WORKS PROGRESS ADMINISTRATION POSTER.]

[*Nos.* 56–58 THE CARNEGIE LIBRARY, BOOKSHELVES, AND BOOKS.]

IN THE CITY OF GOLD ... APPLETON ... APPLETON

AND HIS SUB-MARINE BOAT ... APPLETON ... APPLETON

AND HIS WIRELESS MESSAGE ... APPLETON ... APPLETON

SWIFT AND HIS SKY RACER ... APPLETON ... APPLETON

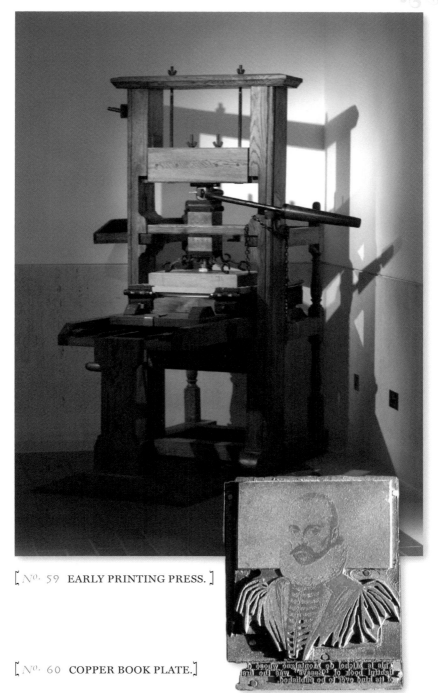

[*N°·* 59 EARLY PRINTING PRESS.]

[*N°·* 60 COPPER BOOK PLATE.]

[*N⁰.* 62 **KITTY IN THE BOOKSTORE.**]

[*Nᵒˢ.* 63–64 **BOOKS.**]

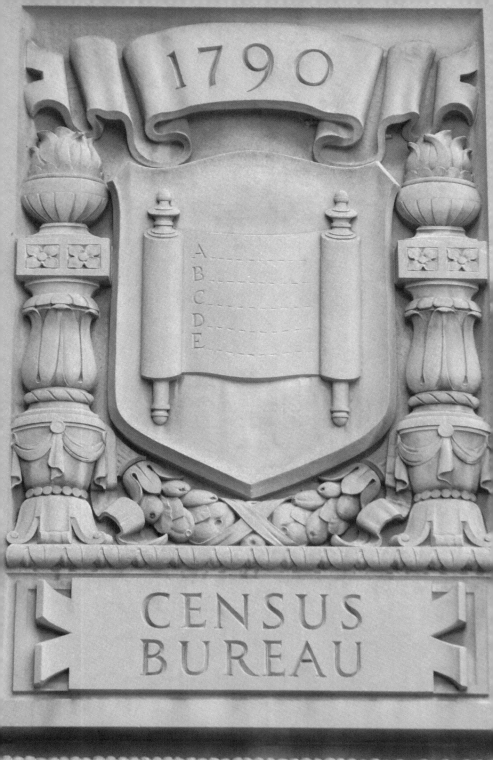

1790

A
B
C
D
E

CENSUS
BUREAU

[*N°.* 65 RELIEF AT THE CENSUS BUREAU, WASHINGTON, D.C.]

[*N°.* 66 LABOR READING, PITTSBURGH, PA.]

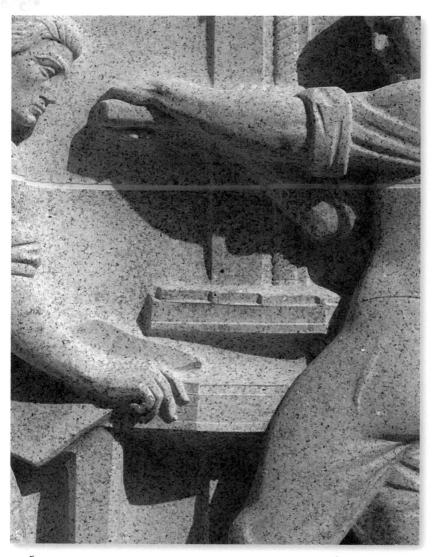

[*N⁰.* 67   PRINTING PRESS DETAIL, WASHINGTON, D.C.]

[*No.* 68 BAS RELIEF AT THE GOVERNMENT
PRINTING OFFICE, WASHINGTON, D.C.]

[*No.* 69 PRINTING A BOOK.]

NOTES &
Sources

[Table of Contents] c. 1899. *Engelhorns Allgemeine Romanbibliothek.* (Engelhorns General Novel Library). Lithograph by Karl Klimsch, c. 1867. (print, poster, color, 79 x 58 cm)

Federal

Page 4. Image No. 1. c. 1900. *The Library of Congress, Washington. West Facade.* Detroit Photographic Co. (photomechanical print mounted on black paper, photochrom, color, image 43 x 53 cm)

Page 4. Image No. 2. *Closed Book with Clasps on the Lap of Robert Ingersoll Aitken's "Past" on the North Side of the National Archives.* By: takomababelot, Flickr.com, Creative Commons.

Page 4. Image No. 3. *Cherub with Open Book on John Donnelly's Bronze Flagpole Base at the Supreme Court (Washington, D.C.).* By: takomababelot, Flickr.com, Creative Commons.

Page 5. Image No. 4. c. 1901. *Library of Congress, Reading Room in Rotunda.* Detroit Photographic Co. (photomechanical print, photochrom, color)

Classic Books and Authors

Page 6. Image No. 5. c. 1630-1655. *Sibyl Holding a Tablet.* Coriolano, Bartolomeo, artist. Reni, Guido, artist. (print, chiaroscuro woodcut, 31 cm x 22 cm)

Page 6. Image No. 6. Sept. 14, 1921. *Gutenberg Bible.* (photographic print)

Page 7. Image No. 7. c. 2007. *Main Reading Room. Portrait Statues of Homer and Plato along the Balustrade. Library of Congress, Thomas Jefferson Building, Washington, D.C.* Highsmith, Carol M., photographer. (photograph, digital, TIFF file, color)

Page 8. Image No. 8. c. 1874. *Moses.* Published and printed by H. Schile, New York. (print, lithograph, hand-colored)

Page 9. Image No. 9. *The Holy Bible Baby.* By: geishaboy500, Flickr.com, Creative Commons.

Page 9. Image No. 10. *Details, Details.* At the ruins of Bara-Gumbad Mosque at Lodhi Gardens—New Delhi, India. By laszlo, Flickr.com, Creative Commons.

Page 10. Image No. 11. c. 1849. *William Shakespeare. Samuel Cousins, A.R.A.* From the Chandos portrait, engraved for the Shakespeare Society, June 1849. Hubbard Collection. (print, mezzotint)

Page 10. Image No. 12. c. 2007. *Main Reading Room. Portrait Statue of Shakespeare along the Balustrade. Library of Congress Thomas Jefferson Building, Washington, D.C.* Highsmith, Carol M., photographer. (photograph, digital, TIFF file, color)

Libraries

Page 11. Image No. 13. c. 1875–1890. *Reading Room of the American Club of Bohemian Ladies, Prague.* Mounted on board. (photographic print, albumen, hand-colored, 6.5 x 10 cm)

Page 11. Image No. 14. c. 1939. *Silence.* Mabel Dwight. Federal Art Project, New York, WPA. (print, lithograph)

Page 12. Image No. 15. c. 1896. *The Reading Room—Bates Hall.* Boston Public Library. Peixotto, Ernest C., artist. (drawing, wash, opaque white and graphite)

Page 13. Image No. 16. *Bookshelves.* By: gadl, Flickr.com, Creative Commons.

Page 14. Image No. 17. c. 1900. *The Public Library of the City of Boston.* Detroit Photographic Co. (photomechanical print, photochrom, color)

Page 14. Image No. 18. c. 1901. *Interior of Bates Hall, Boston Free Library.* C.H. Graves, Universal Photo Art Co., Philadelphia, Pa. (photographic print on stereo card, stereograph)

Page 15. Image No. 19. c. 1908. *New York Public Library, New York.* Detroit Publishing Co. (negative, glass, 3.5 x 5.5 in.)

Page 15. Image No. 20. c. 1930–1950. *Woman at Main Reading Room Card Catalog in the Library of Congress.* Jack Delano. (photographic print)

Civil War

Page 16. Image No. 21. March 12, 1864. *Reading the News—Off Duty.* Rappahannock Station. Edwin Forbes. (drawing, pencil)

Page 16. Image No. 22. c. 1865. *President A. Lincoln Reading the Bible to His Son.* Retouched and photographed by A. Berger, Brooklyn. Published by W. Schaus, New York. (photographic, print, albumen)

Page 16. Image No. 23. c. 1840–1860. *Unidentified Woman Holding Book, with Books on Table to Her Right.* (photograph, sixth-plate daguerreotype, hand-colored)

Page 17. Image Nos. 24–25. c. 1866. *Gardner's Photographic Sketchbook of the War.* Alexander Gardner. Washington, D.C. Philp & Solomons, Washington, D.C.

Children

Page 18. Image No. 26. *Old Kids' Books.* By: Playingwithbrushes. Flickr.com, Creative Commons.

Page 18. Image Nos. 27–28. *Happy Reader Mascaron A Sprinkler Alarm & Monocled Reader Mascaron, New York.* By: takomababelot, Flickr.com, Creative Commons.

Page 19. Image No. 29. *Detail from Gail Sherman Corbett's Bronze Door to City Hall (Springfield, Mass.)*. By: takomababelot, Flickr.com, Creative Commons.

Page 19. Image No. 30. c. 1874. *God Bless Our School*. Published by Currier & Ives, 125 Nassau St., New York. (print, lithograph, hand-colored)

Page 20. Image No. 31. c. 1879. *Two Young Girls Reading Book*. P.O. Vickery. (print, chromolithograph)

Readers

Page 21. Image No. 32. c. 1900. *Old Woman Reading a Book*. The Misses Selby, New York. (photographic print, platinum, 15.7 x 11.4 cm mounted on cream mat, 34.4 x 26.1 cm)

Page 21. Image No. 33. c. 1750–1770. *Woman Reading a Book (Eloyse et Abailard)]*. F. Boucher in del. Paris, chez Demarteau. By Gilles Demarteau. (print, col. crayon manner)

Page 21. Image No. 34. *Reading Man Detail, George F. Fishman's 1991 Mosaic, "Faces Of Flower Avenue" (Silver Spring, Md.)*. By: takomabibelot, Flickr.com, Creative Commons.

Page 22. Image No. 35. c. 1909. *"Dig."* Sadie Wendell Mitchell. Close, Graham, & Scully, Inc., New York. (print, chromolithograph, 22.5 x 14 in.)

Page 23. Image No. 36. c. 1899. *The Library*. Charles Locke. (print, lithograph)

Page 23. Image No. 37. *Studying Homeopath: Bas Relief Detail of Charles Henry Niehaus' 1900 Doctor Samuel Hahnemann Memorial at Scott Circle (Washington, D.C.)*. By: takomabibelot, Flickr.com, Creative Commons.

Page 23. Image No. 38. c. 1910. *De Hollandsche Revue*. Amst[erdam], Steendr, Senefelder. Caspel, Johann Georg van, artist. (print, poster, lithograph, color, 76.2 x 104.2 cm)

Page 24. Image No. 39. c. 1912. *Blind: The Braille Alphabet at Library for the Blind, Institute of the Blind*. Harris & Ewing, photographer. (negative, glass, 5 x 7 in. or smaller)

Page 24. Image No. 40. c. 1907. *Helen Keller, 1880–1968*. (photographic print)

Advertisements

Page 25. Image No. 41. c. 1898. *Stirring Times in Austria Described by Mark Twain in Harper's March*. Harper & Brothers, New York. (print, poster, lithograph, color, 39 x 31 cm)

Page 26. Image No. 42. c. 1899. *Uncle Tom's Cabin*. Courier Litho. Co., Buffalo, N.Y. (print, poster, lithograph, color, 72 x 53 cm.)

Page 27. Image No. 43. c. 1897. *Cinderella*. W.B. Conkey Co., Chicago–New York. Copyright by W.B. Conkey Co. (print, chromolithograph)

Bookstores

Page 28. Image No. 44. c. 1909. *Old Corner Bookstore, First Brick Building in Boston*. Detroit Publishing Co. (photographic print)

Page 28. Image No. 45. *You know it's a good bookstore when...* By: Ben+Sam, Flickr.com, Creative Commons.

Page 29. Image No. 46. c. 1896. *The Bookman—April.* James Montgomery Flagg, artist. New York. (print, poster, lithograph, color)

Page 30. Image No. 47. c. 1925–1930. *Old Man Reading Bible in Wicker Chair on Farmhouse Porch.* Photo by USDA Extension Service. (photographic print)

Religious

Page 30. Image No. 48. c. 1809. *Title Page of a Christmas Book for Little Boys, a Collection of Conversations; the 3rd Virginia Children's Book; illus. with Boy and Woman Seated and Evidently Conversing.* Illus. in PZ32.C5 [Rare Book RR], Library of Congress.

Page 31. Image No. 49. c. 1925. *Religious Books Build Character.* Adolph Treidler. (print, poster, lithograph, color, 53 x 34 cm)

Early 1900s

Page 32. Image No. 50. c. 1910s. *Take Along a Book.* Color lithograph by M. Norstad. (print, poster, color, 53 x 34 cm)

Page 33. Image No. 51. 1920s. *America's Making Told in Books.* Michael Gross Co., New York. (print, poster, color, 54 x 35 cm)

Page 34. Image No. 52. *"Hey Fellows!" Your Money Brings the Book We Need When We Want It.* American Library Association, United War Work Campaign, Week of November 11, 1918. John Sheridan, artist. Committee on Public Information, Division of Pictorial Publicity. (print, poster, lithograph, color, 76 x 51 cm)

Page 35. Image No. 53. c. 1918–1923. *Books Wanted for Our Men in Camp and Over There. Take Your Gifts to the Public Library.* C. B. (Charles Buckles), Falls. (print, poster, color)

Page 36. Image No. 54. c. 1936–1940. *Be Kind to Books Club. Are You a Member?* Arlington Gregg. WPA Illinois Art Project, Chicago, Ill. (print on board, poster, silkscreen, color)

Page 37. Image No. 55. c. 1936–1940. *Little Miss Muffet...Reading a Picture Book.* Arlington Gregg. WPA Illinois Art Project, Chicago, Ill. (print on board, poster, silkscreen, color)

Photographs

Page 38. Image No. 56. *Free to the People, Pittsburgh, Pa. (Carnegie Library).* By takomabibelot, Flickr.com, Creative Commons.

Page 39. Image No. 57. *Library Books.* By: timetrax23, Flickr.com, Creative Commons.

Page 40. Image No. 58. *Vintage Tom Swift Books Detail.* By: adobemac, Flickr.com, Creative Commons.

Page 41. Image No. 59. *Screw Printing Press in a British Library Hallway (London, England).* By: takomabibelot, Flickr.com, Creative Commons.

Page 41. Image No. 60, *Copper Printing Plates—Set 3.* By: Mrs. Gemstone, Flickr.com, Creative Commons.

Page 42. Image No. 61. *Purpose.* By: Striatic, Flickr.com, Creative Commons.

Page 43. Image No. 62. *Kitty at Shakespeare Books.* By: austinevan, Flickr. com, Creative Commons.

Page 44. Image No. 63. *Stockholm Public Library.* By: elmindreda, Flickr. com, Creative Commons.

Page 45. Image No. 64. *Books.* By: gadl, Flickr.com, Creative Commons.

Page 46. Image No. 65. 1790, *A... B... C... D... E...,* Census Bureau, James Earle Fraser's Limestone Relief Panel, Department of Commerce Building, Washington, D.C. By: takomabibelot, Flickr.com, Creative Commons.

Page 47. Image No. 66. *Detail, Daniel Chester French's 1904 Bronze, Labor Reading, Pittsburgh, Pa.* By: takomabibelot, Flickr.com, Creative Commons.

Page 48. Image No. 67. *Printing Press Detail, Carl Paul Jennewein's Trylon, Washington, D.C.* By: takomabibelot, Flickr.com, Creative Commons.

Page 49. Image No. 68. *Government Printing Office Building, Number Four Jackson Alley, Cast Concrete Presswork Bas Relief (Washington, D.C.).* By: takomabibelot, Flickr.com, Creative Commons.

Page 50. Image No. 69. *Printing Press.* By: Herkie, Flickr.com, Creative Commons.

Cover

[Front Cover] c. 1909. *"Dig."* Sadie Wendell Mitchell. Close, Graham, & Scully, Inc., New York. (print, chromolithograph, 22.5 x 14 in.)

[Back Cover] c. 1910s. *Take Along a Book.* Color lithograph by M. Norstad. (print, poster, color, 53 x 34 cm)

LaVergne, TN USA
11 November 2009
163812LV00001B